The Power of Relationships

By

Lee E. Thomas

Scripture quotations are from the
King James Version of the Bible.

Printed in the United States of America

TABLE OF CONTENTS

CHAPTER 1

THE POWER OF RELATIONSHIPS

Oscar Thompson says, "The most important word in the English language is *relationship*." Myron Rush says, "Every problem in the history of mankind is a *people* problem." Whether or not we agree with these strong, dogmatic statements, we must understand that relationships exert great **power** in our lives. Too many times we take the *positive* power for granted, and may not even be aware of the *negative* power until a troubling or broken relationship wreaks much havoc and heartache in our lives. Consider the power of relationships.

In the *physical* realm, relationships are so powerful, they multiply our **EFFECTIVENESS**. Listen to the Lord's assessment of those building a city and a tower that would be called Babel: "Behold, the *people is one*, and they have *all one language*; and this they begin to do: and now nothing will be restrained from them, which they have imagined to do." (Genesis 11:6) What an incredibly amazing statement that God Himself makes concerning the power of *unity*.

This same truth also applies to the Church. God designed the church as *one body*, requiring the individual members to work together in order to make it powerful and effective in the world. Read First Corinthians 12, to get a more comprehensive view of the Church as *His body*.

Perhaps the most powerful aspect of our human relationships is **spiritual**. They reflect the true depth of our spirituality and they profoundly affect our relationship with God. I would ask that you prayerfully meditate on the following ways our relationships impact us in the spiritual realm.

First of all, a broken relationship can **nullify** our prayers. God told Israel, "When ye make many prayers, I will *not* hear: your hands are full of blood." (Isaiah 1:15)

Forgiveness is a key element in the Lord's prayer. Matthew 6:12 says, "And forgive us our debts **AS** we forgive our debtors." If we refuse to forgive others, neither will God forgive us (Matthew 6:14-15). And our prayers will not be answered.

Several years ago I was in Huntington, West Virginia, teaching on prayer. I made the statement that if we had unforgiveness toward anyone, our prayers would be null and void. After the service, a lady, weeping profusely, told me that she had **NEVER** had a single prayer answered. Then she said, "I never knew *why* until tonight." She then confessed that she hated her parents. I asked her if she had taken care of that during the service. The big smile that lit up her face conveyed the answer.

The husband/wife relationship is particularly sweet to the Lord. He calls us *"heirs together* of the grace of life." So, He wants the spousal relationship to be good so that our "prayers be not hindered." (First Peter 3:7)

In Matthew 5:44, the Lord **commands** us to *love* our enemies, bless those who curse us, *do good* to those that hate us, and *pray* for those who despitefully use us and persecute us. If we are to treat our enemies like this, **HOW MUCH MORE** should we treat the one we pledged to "love and cherish 'til death do us part?"

So, how does a broken relationship keep our prayers from being answered? The answer is found in Galatians 5:6, "faith works by (*dia*) love." *Dia* is the channel through which something flows. Without love, faith has no channel or opportunity to work. Conversely, much love provides a larger channel for faith to operate!

This is such a crucial truth for us to understand, I want to use a simple illustration to help secure it in our minds. Think of a brand new, expensive automobile **without** *tires* and *wheels*. Just as that automobile cannot go anywhere without tires and wheels, faith *cannot* work without **LOVE**!!!

Secondly, relationships **regulate our worship**. We may deal rather glibly with our relationships, but not God. Our relationships are so important to Him that He will not even receive our worship if our relationships are in disarray.

Point of reference: our idea of relationship is primarily of family members or those we associate with on a fairly regular basis. However, God's idea of relationship includes *all mankind*!! This is a crucial truth to understand.

David wanted to build a magnificent temple for the *worship* of God, but God said to him, "Thou hast shed blood abundantly, and hast made great wars: thou shalt not build an house unto my name, *because* thou hast shed much blood upon the earth in my sight." (First Chronicles 22:8)

God refused to allow David to build Him a place of worship because he had killed so many people. And God's plan was for His house of worship to be "an **house** of **prayer** for **ALL PEOPLE**." (Isaiah 56:7)

Acts 17:26 declares that God, "Hath made of **one blood** *all nations of men* for to dwell on all the face of the earth...." In heaven there will be neither national nor ethnic groups: we will all be one in Christ. The Lord wants us to treat each other that way **NOW**!!

Giving is one of the higher forms of worship. God loves cheerful givers (Second Corinthians 9:7) and mightily blesses those who do (Luke 6:38). But listen to what Jesus says concerning giving and relationships.

"Therefore if thou bring thy gift to the altar, and there rememberest that thy brother hath ought against thee; leave there thy gift before the altar, and go thy way; **first** *be reconciled* to thy brother, and then come and offer thy gift." (Matthew 5:23-24) The Lord is telling us that we must *first* get our relationships right before He will receive our worship of giving. This is also true for *every* other form of worship.

Thirdly, our relationships determine our **nearness to God**. Jesus called the scribes and Pharisees hypocrites saying, "Their heart is far from me." (Mark 7:6) This refers to *spiritual*, not *physical* proximity. Likewise, if we do not agree with God and His Word, then our heart is also far from Him.

Perhaps the most accurate barometer measuring our nearness to God is our relationships. John puts it like this, "If a man say, I love God, and hateth his brother, he is a liar: for he that loveth not his brother whom he hath seen, how can he love God whom he hath not seen? And this commandment have we from him, That he who loveth God love his brother also." (First John 4:20-21)

The Greek word for brother is not just referring to a family member or to a fellow-believer, but rather to **all mankind**. God wants us to see others as He sees them. Look at Acts 17:25-29, "He giveth to all life, and breath, and all things; and hath made of one blood all nations of men...For in him we live and move, and have our being...we are the *offspring of God....*"

When Jesus told His disciples that they had seen the Father, they didn't understand. So, He simply said, "He that hath seen me hath seen the Father." (John 14:9) Similarly, the phrase, "he that loveth not his brother whom he hath *seen*," is not referring to physically seeing a particular person. Rather, it is knowing that every person in the world is the offspring of God, making all of us brothers!

The Merriam-Webster dictionary defines relationship as "the way in which two or more people or things are *connected*." Since all mankind is connected as the offspring of God, technically we have a relationship with everyone, even those who hate or harm us. Read and meditate on Matthew 5:38-48, for a better understanding of this Biblical concept.

Because of pride, we find it extremely difficult to live this out in everyday life. Consequently, bitterness creeps in, putting us in the position of being "far from God" in our heart.

Not only that, but bitterness is a *root* which continues to grow, producing much bitter fruit, troubling us, and defiling many (Hebrews 12:15).

I told Barbara's story in our book, *Living the Exceedingly Victorious Life*, which deals with strongholds in Christians. Since her story is a classic example of how broken relationships produce bitterness, alienating us from God, I must share it here.

Barbara's husband is a pastor, and I was preaching a revival meeting in their church. After the first evening service, we were fellowshipping in their home, and Barbara said, "I need to tell you my story." She told me how as a pastor's wife she had no peace or joy and did not like being around God's people (which is not a good characteristic for a pastor's wife). One day, she said to God, "Something is wrong with me. Will you show me what it is?"

Now Barbara had missed the entire seventh year of school. She could not make herself get on the school bus. She said, "Daddy broke seventeen limbs on me." (He whipped her seventeen different times trying to make her get on the school bus, but she wouldn't.) She didn't know why she couldn't get on the bus; she just knew she couldn't, so she missed that entire year.

After she asked the Lord to reveal her problem, she had a dream. In her dream, she was being molested by her school bus driver when she was in the sixth grade. She had this same dream more than once, so she shared it with her husband. He said, "God is showing you something." In reality her school bus driver had molested her, and now she began to vividly remember all the details. Consequently, she **hated** him for what he had done to her.

Her husband said, "You've got to forgive him." She said, "I can't forgive him." And they argued back and forth: "You must forgive him" - "I can't forgive him" - "He ruined my life." This rocked on for quite some time until one day, after the standard argument, she jumped up angrily, got into her car and drove away. She ended up at the cemetery where her dad was buried. She said. "Lee, I got out of my car, walked over to my dad's grave, knelt, and forgave him for all the beatings. Then I explained to him why I could not get on the school bus."

She said, "When I got up to leave, I noticed buried next to my dad was the man who had molested me. God said, 'Barb, go next door.' So I knelt by his grave and forgave him for what he did to me. Tears of joy flooded my cheeks. And now, I have peace and joy, and I love God's people."

The bitterness had been there all the time, but she was not aware of it. And, yet, this bitterness kept her from enjoying the joy and peace of God for all those years. Since we can be no nearer to God than we are to any person - living or dead - the devil works overtime trying to get us crossways with each other.

Fourthly, broken relationships greatly **obstruct effective evangelism**. Since the Church is God's appointed instrument to win the world, He is particularly concerned about our treatment of each other as Christians.

Can you feel the pathos of the Lord's heart as He prays, "That they all may be one; as thou, Father, art in me, and I in thee, that they also may be one in us: *that the world may believe* that thou hast sent me." (John 17:21) Disunity in the Church is a powerfully detrimental impediment to soul-winning, but so is **every other broken relationship**!!

To illustrate this truth, I must tell you my story. It began several years ago as the result of a doctor's bill that I refused to pay. The doctor performed a minor surgery that was a complete fiasco. The whole thing was such a failure and so totally unnecessary that the hospital administrator dropped the hospital charges.

Before I moved to a different town, I went to this doctor's office to talk to him about the bill, but I couldn't get in to see him. After I settled into my new church field, I began to pray for God's power to win souls. Each time I cried out for more of God's power, He would say, "What about that doctor bill?"

During this time I had heard that the doctor had gotten into trouble with the government due to Medicare fraud, and I lost track of him. So when I would pray for power, and the Lord would say, "What about that doctor bill?" I would respond with, "Lord, he was a quack and a crook, so I shouldn't have to pay that bill." But I never got God's power. So after a while I would cry out again, "God, I need your power to win souls." And every time He would respond, "What about that doctor bill?" And I would answer, "Lord, he was a quack and a crook; I shouldn't have to pay that bill."

This kind of interplay rocked on for several months, but I never received God's power to win souls. Then I decided to teach my people how to win souls using Oscar Thompson's book, *Concentric Circles of Concern*. The paradigm, of course, was based on the idea of concentric circles. Concentric circles have a common center with each succeeding circle getting larger and farther away from the center. For example, the growth rings in a tree are concentric circles.

Dr. Thompson's first circle represents self, the second circle represents your immediate family, the third circle represents extended family, and so on until you get to person X, someone you don't even know. After studying this paradigm, I decided to skip circle number one, for after all, I am saved, and go straight to circle number two, the immediate family.

So, now I am studying and preparing to teach circle number two as my first presentation. During this process the Lord spoke to me and said, "What about circle number one?" I was so taken aback that I responded with, "What about circle number one?" He said, "What about that doctor bill?"

Finally, I understood - God was not going to give me

His power to win souls, nor was He going to allow me to teach others how to win souls until I dealt with circle number one - self. I said, "Lord, I'll pay the doctor bill." No more excuses, no more delays, just obedience to Him.

Within hours of telling God I would pay the bill, a pastor I did not know invited me to preach a revival meeting in his church. The revival offering was the **exact** amount of the doctor's bill. I gladly paid it, and received God's power too!!

Probably hundreds of times since then, I have said, "Lord, if I had only known I could have had your power for a few hundred dollars, I would have paid the bill a long time ago." I believe that it was the very year following this incident that I baptized sixty-seven people, the most I had ever baptized in a year.

God absolutely refused to give me power to win souls until I took care of that doctor bill. In my mind, I was justified by not paying the bill. I didn't see it as a broken relationship. I saw it as a case of bad doctoring. But God did not agree with my assessment of the situation.

Pride, not poverty, kept me from paying that doctor bill. Pride is almost *always* the culprit in preventing us from getting our broken relationships healed!! Please take care of your broken relationships *now*, so that God can use you mightily in the winning of souls.

Approximately **58 million** souls go to hell every year. We must **NOT** allow broken relationships to hinder our efforts to win them to Christ.

Fifthly, our relationships are eternally powerful, for they will be a major **criterion for judgment**. Jesus said, "For I was an hungred, and ye gave me meat: I was thirsty, and ye gave me drink: I was a stranger and ye took me in: Naked and ye clothed me: I was sick and ye visited me: I was in prison, and ye came unto me. Then shall the righteous answer him saying, Lord, when saw we thee an hungred, and fed thee? or thirsty, and gave thee drink...And the King shall answer and say unto them, Verily I say unto you, In as much as ye have done it unto one of the least of these my brethren, ye have done it unto me." (Matthew 25:35-40)

The Bible mentions multiple judgments. So, as a point of clarity I want to explain *three* of these that affect all of us as Christians.

We *were* judged as **SINNERS** at Calvary. But Jesus took our judgment for us. When He died on the cross, He died *for* us and *as* us. Consider these precious verses:

- (Isaiah 53:6) "...the Lord hath laid on him the iniquity of us all."

- (Second Corinthians 5:21) "For he hath made him to be sin for us, who knew no sin; that we might be made the righteousness of God in him."

- (First Peter 2:24) "Who his own self bare our sins in his own body on the tree...."

Since Jesus was judged and punished by death for all of our sins at Calvary, we can never be charged with any of them again. The **double jeopardy** rule written in the Fifth Amendment of the U.S. Constitution provides the same protection for criminals. Absolutely no one can be convicted more than once for the same offense.

When we accept Jesus as our Saviour, we also accept His payment for all of our sins. Therefore, we can **NEVER** be charged for any sin we commit *after* we are born again. All of our sins are covered by His blood once and for all!!!

As Christians, we are *presently* being judged as **SONS**. As sons of God, He gives us the option of judging ourselves. First Corinthians 11:31-32 says, "For if we would judge ourselves, we should not be judged. But when we are judged, we

9

are chastened (*child training*) of the Lord, that we should not be condemned with the world."

If we refuse to deal with sin in our lives by confessing it and receiving God's forgiveness and cleansing (First John 1:9), then God has no other choice than to *chasten* us. Chasten means "to train a child." He is training us to be conformed to the image of Christ.

Sometimes parents discipline their children by taking their prized possessions. God does the same with us. Because of sin in our lives He may take our *joy* (Psalm 51:12), our *health* (First Corinthians 11:30), our *financial well-being* (Amos 4:6-9), our *family* (Second Samuel 12:14), and even our *lives* (First Corinthians 11:30) (First John 5:16).

When we die, we *shall be* judged as **SERVANTS**. First Corinthians 3:5-11 explains this very well. Six times in this passage Paul talks about labour, labourers, and work. We will be judged according to how we served the Lord here on earth. Sin is never mentioned in this passage.

We are responsible for doing the individual work God has appointed to each of us. However, He wants all of us to treat **EVERY PERSON** we meet as if that person is Jesus. Make no mistake about it, we shall be judged according to how we treat others. Therefore, we should highly value all of our relationships.

CHAPTER 2

THE RELATIONSHIP CYCLE

There are two basic principles that will help us maintain healthy relationships: the **relationship cycle** and the **temperaments**. These are critical *keys* in human behavior. Understanding them will certainly help us create positive relationships. If we don't know them, we will have difficulty trying to "fix" our relationship problems.

I want to illustrate this truth with a personal story. In college, me and my best friend, Charlie Carlisle, majored in engineering which requires advanced math. *Calculus* was one of those courses. Calculus is widely regarded as a very difficult subject - and it is!!! If you google *calculus problems*, you will see what I mean.

Our professor would lecture on eight to ten problems before each test, but the test would include only one or two problems. Charlie and I would choose the two problems we felt he had emphasized in class and we would memorize everything we needed to know in order to solve those two problems. We usually chose the right problems, so we made good grades on the tests. However, we were learning only about 20%, so we didn't **KNOW** calculus!!

The next semester I took a physics course. The first day of class the professor said, "This is the hardest undergraduate course in the entire university." After the first week, I knew he was telling the truth.

He would give us a problem to solve, but you had to *know calculus* in order to solve the problem. And I didn't know calculus. I dropped the course after the first week.

Since **LIFE'S BOTTOM LINE** is relationships, it is absolutely imperative that we learn the basics. **42%** of first marriages end in divorce, **60%** of *second* marriages end in divorce, and **73%** of *third* marriages end in divorce simply because we don't know how to solve the relationship *riddle*!!!

Relationship principles work for **ALL** relationships. Although I want to focus primarily on marital relationships in this chapter, the cycle covers them all.

A brief overview of the broken relationship between King David and his son Absalom provides an excellent example of the relationship cycle going *full circle*. Read Second Samuel 13-18 and note each event that eventually culminates in the final separation of father and son.

Study this chapter until you recognize the cycle in your relationships. Then you can correct the problem before too much damage is done.

Genesis 1 tells the creation story. Genesis 1:31 says, "And God saw **every thing** that He had made, and, behold, it was *very good*...."

The masterpiece of all God's creation was a man made in His own image. He had already proclaimed that every thing He had made was very good. But after He made man He declared that something was wrong. He said, "It is **NOT** good that the man should be alone; I will make him an **help meet** (*ezer*) for him." (Genesis 2:18)

EZER is found 22 times in the Old Testament. Fifteen times *ezer* refers to God helping Israel or those in need. Psalm 121:2 says, "My help (*ezer*) cometh from the Lord, which made heaven and earth." The inference is that since God made *heaven* and *earth*, He can certainly help us in any situation we face.

Look at God's mercy and grace in Hosea 13:9, "O Israel, thou hast **destroyed** thyself, but in **me** is thine help (*ezer*)." Destroyed refers primarily to *moral corruption* but could include *physical destruction* as well. God is offering to take care of their situation which they caused and make the nation whole again.

Other than sending Christ to die for our sins, establishing relationships for us was the greatest thing God ever did for mankind. Many times we fail to recognize this until it is too late!!

Second Samuel 13-18 tells us the story of the shattered relationship between King David and his son Absalom. In the final chapter of their broken relationship, Absalom tries to steal the kingship of Israel from his father. In his attempt to kill his own father, he himself is killed by Joab, David's general.

When David hears the news of Absalom's death, he weeps, and mourns, and grieves for his son. He cries out, "O my son Absalom, my son, my son Absalom! Would God I had died for thee, O Absalom, my son, my son!"

In this moment he realizes that his son was much more important than his kingdom. He would have gladly given up his kingdom for his son's life.

Many times men will allow their business to replace their family in importance. Under the guise of *providing* for the family, the business consumes the time, effort, and love that belongs to the wife and kids. In a matter of time the marriage is hollow with the homelife just a shell for show. The intimacy in the marriage is gone and the kids have moved on to something else, realizing their dad is more interested in his business and his money than he is in them.

Dads, you must realize that your children would a million times over rather have your time and affection than the material things you provide. Please don't wait until you too will be crying with David, "My child, my child, would God I had died for thee."

Since establishing relationships for us is the second greatest thing God ever did, it is absolutely imperative that we understand as much as we can about *how* relationships *work*! Being familiar with the relationship **CYCLE** will give insights concerning relationship situations you may encounter.

All relationships - marital, family, employer/employee, friends, etc. - tend to follow this pattern. Since marriage was the very first relationship God instituted and the one that causes the most heartaches, we will be primarily referring to it throughout this chapter.

Perhaps the very first principle we need to understand is that all relationships are based on **personal needs**. The employer/employee is a perfect example: the employee needs money to live and the employer needs someone to work to help him make money.

Two people become friends if, for no other reason than that they enjoy each other's companionship. That companionship strengthens their corporate ability. Ecclesiastes 4:9-10 says, "Two are better than one; because they have a good reward for their labour. For if they fall, the one will lift up his fellow: but woe to him that is alone when he falleth; for he hath not another to help him up."

<u>The Relationship Cycle</u>

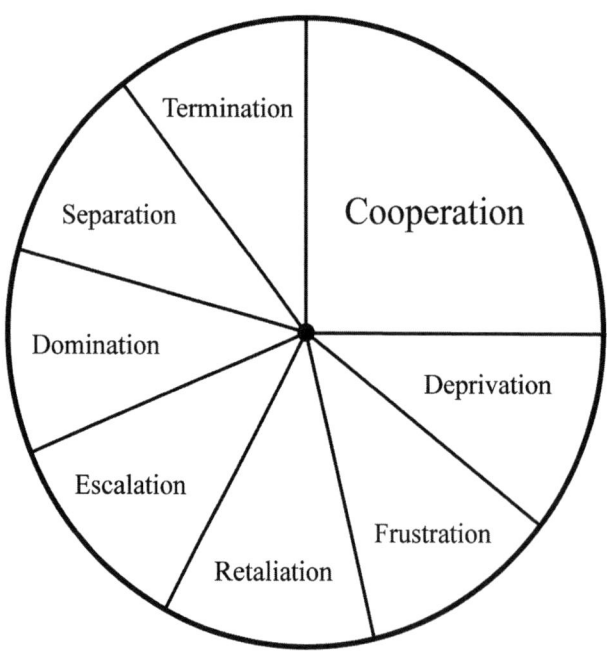

COOPERATION

Since all relationships revolve around *personal needs*, we must **cooperate** to meet each other's needs. I have an evangelist friend who claims that *sex* and *money* (the **lack** of each) are the only problems in marriage. There are probably others, but these two certainly loom large.

Wives need a sense of *security*, and money helps provide that for her. They also need to feel *loved*. God commands husbands to love their wives "as Christ also loved the church, and gave himself for it." (Ephesians 5:25)

Love is basically *meeting needs*. Communication is literally the life-blood of relationships because this is how we discover each others needs. Communication involves much more that just talking, it includes listening intently, and striving to understand what is really being said.

When I began a full-time itinerant ministry in 2004, my wife told me that we needed a home security system. We lived at the end of a dead-end street with almost no traffic; so I said that we really didn't need a security system. You see, what she *said* was, "We need a security system." But what she *meant* was, "I am afraid to stay by myself when you are gone."

I only heard what she said, **NOT** what she meant. So, if your spouse says something that doesn't seem to make sense to you, probe with questions until you understand. That is **communication!!**

Husbands need *support*, *respect*, and *affection* from their wives. So, God made Adam an "help-meet" (*ezer*). Ezer means to *help* and to *succour*. Succour involves assistance and support in times of hardship and distress.

God knew that life on earth would not be easy for mankind. Job 5:7 says, "Yet man is born unto *trouble*, as the sparks fly upward." Jacob told Pharoah, "...*few* and *evil* have the days of the years of my life been." (Genesis 47:9)

Israel brought most of their troubles upon themselves by worshiping idols and turning away from God. But God kept being their *ezer* anyway. Sometimes as husbands, we do stupid things, but we need you ladies to be our *ezer* anyway!!

Husbands also need **respect**. First Peter 3:1-6 presents a godly lifestyle for wives designed by God to win lost husbands to Christ. If this lifestyle is able to save lost husbands, how much more will it bless Christian husbands.

Verse six declares that "Sara obeyed Abraham, calling him Lord...." She did this even though he turned her over to King Abimelech for sexual pleasure (Genesis 20).

Husbands also need **affection**. We are told to love our wives with *agape* love - love from the heart like Christ loves the Church. But in Titus 2:4, wives are *taught* to love (*philandros*) their husbands. This kind of love is from the head, and means to be affectionate. It is also translated in Mark 14:44 as *kiss*. So, wives are to be showing affection, and kissing their husbands.

Through communication we will discover other needs of our spouses. The main idea is to meet each other's needs whatever they may be.

DEPRIVATION

When our needs are **NOT** being met, we experience **emotional deprivation**. We become emotionally drained for something only the spouse can supply.

We feel rejected by the one we love which may also produce low self-esteem. This often results in self-pity and even depression. However, as soon as our needs are being fulfilled again, these kind of feelings dissipate very quickly.

The goal at this point is for the relationship to return to cooperation - meeting each other's needs. Before the relationship gets to the next negative stage we must try two helpful solutions - the **golden rule** and **communication**.

The golden rule is found in Matthew 7:12, which tells us to do unto others **AS** we would have them do unto us. The golden rule is pro-active; we do good things to others *first*! Many times our acts of love and kindness to our spouses will be reciprocated.

Try communication!! Don't suffer in silence. **COMMUNICATION** is one of the major rules of healthy relationships. Just talking to our spouses about the situation could very well solve the problem. Too many times our own pride prevents us from doing this, so we continue to suffer: **COMMUNICATE, COMMUNICATE, COMMUNICATE!!!**

FRUSTRATION

The next stage in the *cycle* is **frustration**. Frustration produces unexpressed anger, irritability, and a desire to shun our spouses as much as possible. Frustration results from focusing on ourselves. So, the best way to get beyond this is to obey Isaiah 26:3, "Thou wilt keep him in perfect peace, whose mind is stayed on thee."

Remaining in this mode will also have a negative impact on our spouses and could very well cause them to respond in kind, making the situation even worse. Not only that, but this attitude could affect our health.

Frustration is basically *unexpressed anger*. According to medical research, our lower backs store most of our *unexpressed anger*. Many people develop severe and debilitating pain in the lumbar region of the back. Chronic stress activates the sympathetic nervous system that puts pressure on the spinal cord.

And on a more somber note, we may be giving the devil an opportunity to get involved in our marriages. Ephesians 4:26-27 says, "Be ye angry, and sin not: let not the sun go down upon your wrath: Neither give place to the devil." Place (*topos*) means opportunity or occasion for acting.

As Christians we should **NEVER** go to bed angry, lest our anger turns to wrath. Wrath is extreme anger with a deep desire to punish the one we blame. This takes us to the next stage of the cycle - *retaliation*!

RETALIATION

Retaliation sparks an emotional war. In this stage we have stopped communicating our needs because we no longer view our spouses as our *ezers* but as our adversaries. Our focus ceases to be self-pity and becomes an intense effort to inflict emotional pain on them.

In the cooperation stage where needs are being met by both parties, the relationship is well and healthy. The next two stages, deprivation and frustration, is common in all marriages to some degree. But the relationship is still healthy because these two stages are fairly easy to fix.

However, *retaliation* is a slippery slope. At this point, the relationship is in serious trouble unless one of the parties is willing to stop the war and obey First Peter 4:8, "Above all things have fervent charity amoung yourselves: for charity shall cover the **multitude of sins**."

There is a story in Aesop's Fables about a contest between the sun and the wind. The one which compelled a man to remove his coat would be the winner. The more forcefully the wind blew, the tighter the man drew his coat around him. The sun began to shine with brightness and warmth. Soon the man removed his coat. This story reveals the power of *gentleness* and *kindness*.

David was perhaps the greatest king in Israel's history. In Second Samuel 22, he wrote a song about God's goodness toward him. In verse thirty-six, he said, "...Thy *gentleness* hath made me **great**."

In all of our relationships, let us shine with *love* and *gentleness* and *kindness*. And maybe, just maybe, all of our relationships will be healthy and strong!!

ESCALATION

Unless one of the partners plays *peacemaker* in the retaliation stage, the emotional war will begin to **escalate**. What was basically a marital skirmish, becomes a full-scale war.

Now, neither partner is having their needs met. Sometimes either or both may explore other relationships. The purpose is two-fold: to get their needs met *and* to aggravate their partner.

Many times one of the partners, usually the wife, gives up the fight for the sake of the kids. She will perfunctorily perform her basic duties as a wife, but the love and affection is long gone! The husband is now getting his needs met to some degree, but he is not fulfilled because he knows his wife is just going through the motions.

This stage is the last *good* chance to save the marriage. In order to do so, one of the partners must obey God's two commands in Romans 12:21, "Be not overcome (*nikao*) of evil, but overcome evil with good."

Nikao means to conquer or to be victorious. Both times in this verse, overcome is in the imperative mood which expresses a *command* to the hearer from the Commander!! We are commanded **NOT** to be conquered by evil, and we are commanded to conquer evil with **good**.

God **NEVER** gives us a command that is impossible to

do. He will give us the grace and power we need to accomplish this as we look to Him. But we must *choose* to do it God's way instead of our way. *Our way won't work*!!

DOMINATION

If the relationship fails to be healed in the escalation stage, we move into the *domination* stage. In war, one party wins and the other loses. Now, the winner begins to dominate the loser.

During this stage, the emotional war may become physical. The winner gloats in victory and may deal in a high-handed way with the loser.

This is the very worst way to relate to others. The loser could very well lose all their self-esteem, feeling like a non-entity in the relationship. A sense of hopelessness sets in and there is no longer any desire whatsoever to forgive the oppressor. And **NO** marriage can survive without forgiveness.

This stage may last for a very long time because the wife hangs around for the kid's sake. She thinks an *unhealthy* home atmosphere is better than a broken home without both parents.

SEPARATION

When the loser can no longer endure being totally dominated, she leaves. An interesting aspect of this **separation** stage is that sometimes she goes back to her oppressor.

Many times the husband will promise to change his ways and plead with her to come back - and she does. But the major reason for her return to an abusive relationship is the *soul-tie* between them.

The one-flesh (*soul-tie*) bond is a *law* designed by God

to make marriages strong. Matthew 19:5-6 says, "For this cause shall a man leave father and mother, and shall *cleave* to his wife: and they twain shall be *one flesh*? Wherefore they are no more twain, but *one flesh*. What therefore God hath joined together, let not man put asunder."

The Greek word for *cleave* means to **glue together**. What God has glued together should not be torn apart. This is why an abused wife will keep returning to her abusive husband. She may return multiple times before she finally calls it quits.

TERMINATION

Finally, the marriage is **terminated** by divorce. In over fifty years of ministry, I have been involved in only one situation where the divorced couple realized they were still in love and wanted me to remarry them.

According to research statistics, *six percent* of divorcees remarry the same person. So, once a relationship it terminated, the odds aren't very good for reconciliation. This is really sad since Christian couples can apply simple Biblical principles to save their marriage.

Since establishing relationships is the second greatest thing God ever did for mankind, we should value them much more highly than we seem to do!! May we all realize how powerful and wonderful are our relationships and act accordingly. May we never learn the hard way that **OUR RELATION-SHIPS ARE MORE IMPORTANT THAN KINGDOMS!!!!**

CHAPTER 3

THE TEMPERAMENTS

The Cambridge Dictionary defines personality as the type of person you are, shown by the way you **behave**, **feel**, and **think**. It is your unique pattern of *behaving*, *feeling*, and *thinking* that distinguishes you from all others.

Personality is so important that many companies administer a personality profile test to prospective employees. This helps to avoid bad hires and reduce employee turnover. Some see a personality test as one of the most important factors in the hiring spectrum.

If personality is such a crucial element in employer/employee relationships, *how much more* in our more intimate relationships of family and friends. Since personalities play such a pivotal role in our lives, we would be wise to become familiar with them.

Although one's personality is shaped by various aspects of life such as race and sex, the singular most powerful factor influencing the personality is temperament. Think of temperament as your **PERSONALITY DNA**. Of the eight billion people in the world, not one has your unique personality!!

Tim LaHaye says, "Temperament influences everything you do - from sleep habits to eating style, to the way you get along with other people. Humanly speaking, there is no other influence in your life more powerful than your temperament or combination of temperaments." (LaHaye 9)

If the temperament is so powerful, what is it? Ole Hallesby says that the temperament is *inborn* and remains throughout life, independent of our conscious being. "From the unconscious it flows continually to influence our conscious lives, asserting itself with instinctive *force* and *tenacity*...We may say that temperament is the soul's **essential response to**

its surroundings." (Hallesby 5-10)

Temperament has absolutely nothing to do with one's *morality* or *spirituality*!! It is totally a soul function. Your soul (*mind, will, emotions*) is who you are as a human being.

Hallesby's description of temperament as the "soul's *essential response* to its surroundings" is spot on. Through our five senses, our souls are constantly being bombarded with tons of *information* and *impressions*. Our reaction to this information and these impressions is determined by our individual temperament. Basically, temperament is a pre-packaged unit of responses to life and relationships.

There are four temperaments - choleric, sanguine, melancholy, and phlegmatic. Three of these directly reflect specific functions of the soul.

The melancholy's response to the impressions of life is *filtered* primarily through the **mind**. Therefore, his response comes only after analysis and contemplation.

The sanguine's response is *filtered* primarily through his **emotions**. His primary emotion is one of joy; hence, he enjoys life. He loves to share his joy with others, so he is usually the life of the party, making people laugh.

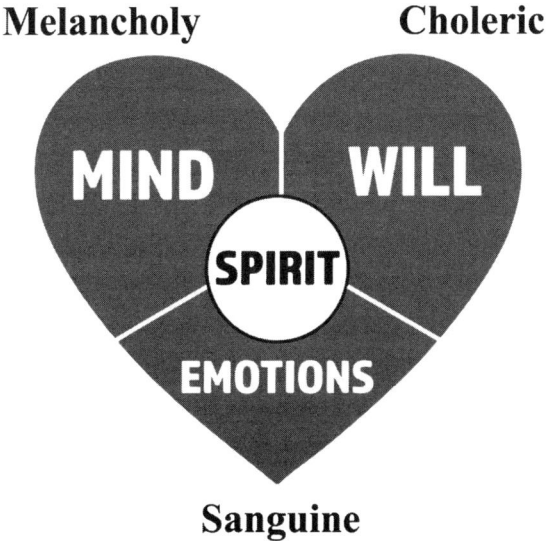

The choleric's response is *filtered* primarily through the **will**. He lives in a practical world and is constantly endeavoring to *conquer* life, whether *goals*, *situations*, or *people*. In order to succeed in these endeavors, he must be in **control** which is his primary characteristic.

The phlegmatic is the most even-keeled temperament, and is not unduly affected by the mind, the will, or the emotions. However, it is still a soul function. He lives in a nonchalant world and basically *accepts* life as it is. He tends to be calm, non-confrontational, tolerant of others, and adaptable to situations.

Temperament comes from a Latin word that means *the right blending*. All of us are a blend or combination of at least two temperaments. However, one will always be predominant. Hence, saying that someone is sanguine simply refers to his predominant temperament.

There are over 1,500 kinds of musical instruments in the world, and yet there are only *twelve notes*. Think of all the beautiful music you have heard coming from twelve notes!! Likewise, the blending of four temperaments produces such a vast variety of personalities that of the eight billion people in the world, no two are the same.

Let's consider some of these combinations. Both cholerics and sanguines are *extroverts*. So, a combination of these two produces a person that is outgoing, optimistic, and outspoken. Both melancholies and phlegmatics are *introverts*. So, a combination of these two produces a person that is introverted, pessimistic, and soft-spoken. These combinations are called *natural* blends.

A choleric/melancholy blend produces a person that is decisive, organized, and goal-oriented. A sanguine/phlegmatic blend produces a person that is easy-going, relaxed, and stable. These combinations are called *complementary* blends because they complement each other. For example, the choleric is driven to accomplish goals while the melancholy is a perfectionist. This combination works well together because the choleric side is driven to accomplish while the melancholy side makes sure it is done right.

A sanguine/melancholy blend produces a person that is both extroverted/introverted, and very emotional. After teaching the relationship seminar in a church in Kentucky, the pastor's wife told me something was wrong with her because she would be laughing one minute and crying the next. There was nothing wrong with her. She was a sanguine/melancholy. This combination is called an *opposite* blend. The other opposite blend is choleric/phlegmatic, producing a person that likes to be in control, and is yet subdued.

Understanding temperaments can certainly enhance our lives and our relationships. Knowing your own temperament with its unique set of strengths and weaknesses helps you accept who you are. Knowing the temperament of your spouse and your children definitely helps you understand *why* they act the way they do.

For example, my youngest son, Johnny, is sanguine. Many times the family would be in the car waiting for him so we could go. Finally, he would emerge from the house with his shoes in his hands. In getting ready to go, he would spend most of his time combing his hair and would not have time to put on his shoes. I thought he was trying to aggravate me, but he wasn't. He was just being himself. Note: I was *not* familiar with the temperaments at that time!!

Since the sanguine basically lives by his emotions, he can easily experience the *joy* and the *pain* of others. This is why he is so widely loved. This gives him the ability to inspire and encourage others. Although Johnny was not the best player on his high school basketball team, he was the **HEART** and **SOUL** of the team.

Running late is another major weakness of many sanguines. They encounter so many interesting things or people on the journey, being on time never even crosses their mind. At one time, Johnny and Andy (his brother) who is phlegmatic, worked for the same company. They rode together for about a week. Since Johnny was late almost every day, Andy said, "You drive your vehicle and I will drive mine."

Johnny graduated from a Christian high school that did something special at graduation to highlight something interesting about their senior year. It just so happens that Johnny was late *54 times* that year. The school put all of his tardy slips in a book and presented it to him at his graduation.

Understanding your spouse's temperament can transform your home. I counseled a couple on the verge of divorce She was phlegmatic, he was choleric. He was so controlling, she couldn't take any more of his verbal abuse. Neither of them knew anything about the temperaments. When I discussed the traits of a choleric personality, he broke down and wept. He had never realized how badly he was treating her. This saved their marriage.

Your spouse's temperament will always be different from yours because *opposites* **attract**. I am a melancholy/phlegmatic while my wife is a sanguine/phlegmatic. Melancholies and sanguines are totally opposite. Her strengths basically covers my weaknesses and my strengths covers her weaknesses. So, opposites also **accentuate**. And they can also **aggravate**. However, since our secondary temperament is phlegmatic, we never have any major fights because we both love peace.

Before I give you a list of temperament traits to help you identify your temperament blend and those of your loved ones, I want to make the **major truth** concerning temperaments abundantly clear: temperament is a soul function, and the soul of man is subservient to his spirit. Therefore, the spirit of man, under the influence of the Holy Spirit can nullify the negative characteristics of his temperament and enhance the positives.

Furthermore, a person filled with the Holy Spirit will be exhibiting the **fruit of the Spirit**, rather than temperament traits. The more Spirit-filled and Spirit-led a person is, the more difficult it is to identify his temperament. This is because your temperament is totally a soul issue, and your soul is **NOT** born again - only your spirit is born again.

Perhaps the best way to identify your temperament is to carefully study the traits of each temperament, choosing those that are applicable. The one with the most traits (both positive and negative) will be the predominant temperament, while the one with the second most will be the secondary.

If there seems to be no clear-cut choice, get someone who knows you really well to take the test for you. Sometimes we find it difficult to be objective about ourselves, especially concerning the negatives.

Following is a list of the four temperaments with their corresponding traits. I think you will find this study interesting, challenging, informative, and rewarding. Studying this in a group setting is also a lot of fun, for others will have insightful comments about your particular temperament.

SANGUINE

STRENGTHS	WEAKNESSES
Carefree	Angers easily
Charming	Controls conversations
Childlike	Craves popularity
Compassionate	Disorganized
Creative	Easily distracted
Curious	Easily influenced
Enjoys life	Easily tempted
Enthusiastic	Egotistical
Friendly	Exaggerates
Funny	Forgetful
Generous	Immature
Happy/Cheerful	Impulsive
Inspires others	Insecure
Magnetic personality	Instability
Optimistic	Interrupts others
Outgoing	Makes excuses
People-oriented	Messy
People skills	Nosy
Perceptive	Restless
Quick to apologize	Superficial
Sincere	Trivia-minded
Sympathetic	Undisciplined
Talkative	Unpredictable
Very demonstrative	Unproductive
Warm	Unreliable
	Weak-willed

CHOLERIC

STRENGTHS	WEAKNESSES
Adventurous/daring	Anger
Competitive	Argumentative
Decisive	Bossy
Excels in emergencies	Can't relax
Focuses on action (a doer)	Crafty/manipulative
Good judge of character	Cruel/sarcastic
Independent	Demanding
Intuitive mind	Domineering
Leader	Frank
Optimistic/positive	Headstrong
Persuasive	Hostile
Practical	Hot-tempered
Problem solver	Impatient
Productive	Insensitive
Resourceful	Narrow-minded
Result-oriented	Opinionated/prejudiced
Self-confident	Proud/haughty
Strong-willed	Rebellious
Tenacious	Reckless
Visionary	Revengeful
	Tactless
	Unaffectionate
	Unapologetic
	Unforgiving
	Unsympathetic/cold
	Violent
	Workaholic

MELANCHOLY

STRENGTHS	WEAKNESSES
Analytical	Critical of others
Artistic	Depression prone
Compassionate	Hard to please
Conscientious	Impractical
Considerate	Inflexible
Creative	Insecure
Deep reasoning power	Introspective
Detailed	Legalistic
Discerns problems	Low self-esteem
Idealistic	Moody
Gifted/genius	Negative
Loyal/faithful	Persecution complex
Perfectionist	Pessimistic
Persistant	Rejects compliments
Planner	Revengeful
Purposeful	Self-centered
Self-disciplined	Sense of unworthiness
Self-sacrificing	Skeptical
Sensitive	Slow to "get started"
Serious	Smileless
Thoughtful	Socially awkward
	Suspicious
	Theoretical
	Touchy
	Unforgiving

PHLEGMATIC

STRENGTHS	WEAKNESSES
STRENGTHS	*WEAKNESSES*

STRENGTHS

Adaptable
Agreeable
Calm under pressure
Competent
Consistant
Cooperative
Dependable
Diplomatic
Easy going
Efficient
Good listener
Inoffensive
Kind
Likable
Mediatorial
Patient
Pleasant
Practical
Quiet
Sympathetic & compassionate
Tolerant
Well balanced
Witty (dry sense of humor)

WEAKNESSES

Aimless
Avoids responsiblility
Bland
Compromising
Dull
Fearful
Indecisive
Indifferent
Lazy
Path of "least resistance"
Self-righteous
Slow
Spectator
Stingy/selfish
Stubborn
Unenthusiastic
Unmotivated

CHAPTER 4

RESTORING RELATIONSHIPS

The Bible paints a very graphic picture of broken relationships. "A brother offended is harder to be won than a strong city: and their contentions are like the bars of a castle." (Proverbs 18:19)

Besieging a strong, fortified city may require a prolonged period of **time** and strenuous **effort**. So, broken relationships may require much work on our part. Too many times we may feel as if the time and effort is **NOT** worth it, so we give up and quit.

Historically, Masada may be the most famous of besieged cities. Approximately 960 Israeli zealots built a fortress there to protest Roman rule in Israel.

The fortress was built on the top of a hill with a very narrow pathway as the only access. So, in order for the Romans to capture the fortress, they built a ramp to the top composed of thousands of tons of rock and soil. This took much time and effort, but they won the battle.

Biblically, the siege of Jerusalem during the reign of King Hezekiah may be the most significant. Hezekiah's testimony was that, "He trusted in the Lord God of Israel; so that after him was none like him among all the kings of Judah, nor any that were before him." (Second Kings 18:5)

So, when the Assyrians besieged Jerusalem, King Hezekiah **prayed** and God sent an angel who killed 185,000 Assyrian soldiers in one night. (Second Kings 19:35) Although, we don't want our broken relationships to end in death for either party, praying about the situation can be very effective!!

Hopefully, our broken relationships can be restored without the intense difficulties of a besieged city or the hopelessness of iron bars protecting a castle. But this Biblical analogy helps us realize the seriousness of the situation. Following are steps we can take to resolve relationship issues.

When a relationship is messed up, both parties may be at fault. Sometimes we *innocently* **say** or **do** something that offends others. They may not say anything about it but their attitude changes toward us. Now we are crossways with each other but we don't know why.

The best response in this situation is to accept personal responsibility for the broken relationship. They think you are at fault whether you do or not.

Proverbs 13:10 says, "**ONLY** by **PRIDE** cometh contention...." Pride is such a devastating sin, it got Lucifer kicked out of heaven. God hates a "proud look" (Proverbs 6:17) and He "resisteth the proud." (First Peter 5:5) Pride will literally destroy your relationship with people and damage your fellowship with God.

Many times our own pride hinders us from accepting responsibility in broken relationships. We must understand that God Himself has *commanded* us to be "clothed with humility." (First Peter 5:5)

Humility means that we don't think about ourselves at all. So, when we are clothed with humility, pride dissipates. Therefore, when we humble ourselves before them, this helps defuse the situation.

Once we accept personal responsibility, the next step is to *ask* for and *give* forgiveness as the case may be. Due to pride, this seems to be very difficult. However, when you do it, God will flood you with His grace. (James 4:6)

Several years ago I was out visiting some of our church members. Two different ladies gave me some fresh green beans. One batch was already washed and snapped, ready to cook. The other had just been picked and had to be washed and snapped. My wife cooked those that had already been prepared but the other bag of beans somehow ended up behind the toaster and we forgot about them.

That Sunday after church, Miss Helen, who gave me the unsnapped beans, asked how they tasted. The ones Sue cooked were very good, so I told Helen, "They were very good." But it wasn't her beans we ate. As a matter of fact, hers molded behind the toaster and we threw them away.

Pride prevented me from telling her that the beans she had given to me spoiled, so I basically lied to her about the beans. God would not even let me preach that night until I got right with Miss Helen. So, I went to her house. She and her husband had company, about a half dozen people. They were all visiting on the back porch. I had to confess before all these people that I, the pastor, had lied to her about the beans. (That will humble you.)

Was she mad or upset with me? NO!!! She forgave me, and gave me another bag of green beans along with some new potatoes. How God's grace flowed that day. He will do the same for you. Don't allow your pride to hurt other people and deprive yourself of God's grace and blessing.

It is fairly easy to forgive someone when they ask for your forgiveness. But to give it *unsought* seems very difficult. Just as God resists the proud, so do we. Therefore, if they are too proud to seek forgiveness, we tend to refuse to give it. But we must not let the devil get the upper hand in those situations. For our sake, for their sake, and for the sake of the Kingdom of God, we must forgive others whether they seek it or not!!

Although forgiveness seems difficult, it is **ESSENTIAL**. Hear what Jesus said, "For if ye forgive men their trespasses, your heavenly Father will also forgive you: But if ye forgive not men their trespasses, neither will your Father forgive your trespasses." (Matthew 6:14-15) This makes forgiveness *serious* business!!

When David became the King of Israel, there was a three-year famine in the land. Since God delights in blessing

His people, David asked the Lord about the famine. "And the Lord answered, It is for Saul, and for his bloody house, because he slew the Gibeonites." (Second Samuel 21:1)

Although David had nothing to do with Saul's evil deed, as king, he had to get right with the Gibeonites. You can read the entire story in Second Samuel 21, but the salient point is that broken relationships between the Israelites and the Gibeonites resulted in a three-year famine for Israel.

Peter asked Jesus, "How oft shall my brother sin **against** me, and I forgive him? Till seven times? Jesus saith unto him, I say not unto thee, Until seven times: but, Until *seventy times seven*." (Matthew 18:21-22) This indicates that forgiveness is basically an **ATTITUDE** rather than an act.

In Luke 17:4, Jesus said that if someone trespasses against you seven times in a day, and each time says, "I repent," you must forgive him. It would seem to us that if someone sinned against us seven times in one day, his repentance would not be real. But Jesus said forgive him anyway.

Forgiveness is really powerful because it reflects the character of God. The **CROSS** is the symbol of that divine love. "But God commendeth his love *toward us*, in that, while we were yet sinners, Christ died for us." (Romans 5:8)

Forgiveness also releases us from the prison of anger, hatred, and bitterness. Every Christian should become familiar with John 20:23, "Whose soever sins ye remit, they are remitted unto them; and whose soever sins ye retain, they are retained."

The Greek word for retain is *krateo*. Krateo means to have dominion over, to rule over, or to be the master. So, if you refuse to forgive someone, for whatever reason, that unforgiven issue will have dominion over you. It will rule over you and be your master. You will be in spiritual prison for the rest of your life. You will be cut off from the peace, the power, and the joy of the Lord.

Are you willing to live the rest of your life in a spiritual junkyard, **UNUSABLE** by God, just because you are either unwilling to forgive or ask for forgiveness? Watchman Nee, one of my favorite authors, was required by God to ask 200 people for forgiveness **BEFORE** God would allow him to write for Him. If God would not use Watchman Nee until he got his relationships right, neither will He use any of us.

If we are serious about restoring relationships, we must be continually committed to meeting their needs. Often, one of the main factors in damaged relationships is **UNMET NEEDS**!!

One of the main needs in everyone's life is **SELF-ESTEEM**. In his book, *I'm OK; You're OK*, Thomas Harris suggests that **96%** of the population has "not OK" feelings about themselves. Joyce Landorf Heatherley believes this results from being inundated with **rejection**, in varying degrees, all of our lives. But when "others discern the good, the noble, the honorable, and the just tenets of our character (no matter how **miniscule** they may be) and then proceed **to tell us** how they admire those traits, we feel visible. We begin to 'see' ourselves and our **worth**. We feel nurtured and nourished, but mostly we feel loved." (Heatherly 10)

We tend to see others as we see ourselves. Those with low self-esteem do not feel good about themselves, consequently, neither do they feel good about others. This is not a good trait for building healthy relationships.

One of my favorite relationship scriptures is Philippians 2:3-4, "...let each **esteem** other better than themselves. **Look** not every man on his own things, but every man also on the things of others."

To *esteem* others means that we **value** them. When we value others, we will treat them with love and respect. *Look* means to **consider**. Therefore, when we see a need in their lives, we automatically meet that need.

Love is one of the most important aspects of restoring a relationship. We must be committed to the kind of love described in First Corinthians 13. This love is so wonderful that it, *"Beareth* all things, *believeth* all things, *hopeth* all things, *endureth* all things." **With** this kind of love **NOTHING ELSE MATTERS**! Love endures a lot of junk!!

This love is all-comprehensive; so much so that **without** it **NOTHING ELSE MATTERS**! Paul says that one could have the gift of *prophecy*, understand **ALL** *mysteries*, have **ALL** *knowledge*, have **ALL** *faith*, and be very *generous*, but without love all these great qualities are absolutely worthless.

Each of us has positive characteristics depending on our particular temperament. Focusing on the positive qualities of others is another step in restoring relationships. This is not only a helpful way to heal relationships but also a good way to treat all people.

Those who are thinking, feeling, and acting negatively toward us usually believe that we feel the same way about them. So, publicly saying good things about them, pointing out good deeds they have done, and complimenting them on character traits you like will be soothing to them. More than that, we should always take the high road in relationships because we are representing our Heavenly Father here on earth.

He wants us to treat others as He does. He says, "Love your enemies, bless them that curse you, do good to them that hate you, and pray for them which despitefully use you, and persecute you; that ye may be the children of your Father which is in heaven: for he maketh his sun to rise on the evil and on the good, and sendeth rain on the just and on the unjust." (Matthew 5:44-45)

We are commanded to give thanks in *everything* (First Thessalonians 5:18). Everything includes both good and bad. Especially in broken relationships we are to express gratitude and appreciation to God for them. This causes any negative feelings we have toward the person to disappear.

Since faith works by love (Galatians 5:6), God now has

an opportunity to work in us and in them. Several years ago I was praying for a certain thing. After three days with no answer from God, I asked Him *why* He wasn't answering my prayer. He led me to Galatians 5:6, "faith worketh by love."

Then He reminded me of a businessman who had made a commitment to financially support our ministry. I was praying for his business and God was blessing it but he wasn't helping us. I wasn't angry at him but I was disappointed. That disappointment was enough to keep God from answering my prayers. I changed my attitude and said to God, "I don't care if he ever sends us anything." And God began to answer my prayers again.

Consequently, the more fervently you love, the more effective your faith will be. In the phrase, "faith worketh **by** love," by (*dia*) denotes the channel of an act. And the larger the channel, the greater the flow. If you want your prayers answered, you **MUST LOVE**!!

One of the greatest things you can do for others is to **pray** for them. If their relationship with you is not good, this provides an even more compelling reason to pray. Jacob's story reveals this wonderful truth.

Jacob basically stole his father's blessing from his twin brother Esau. As a result, Esau swore to kill him. So Jacob fled to his uncle Laban's house. He married two of Laban's daughters, and God blessed him there.

After twenty years (Genesis 31:40), God instructed Jacob to return to Israel. Jacob sent messengers to Esau to tell him he was coming home. They returned with the news that Esau and 400 men were coming to meet them.

When Jacob heard this, he was "greatly afraid and distressed." (Genesis 32:7) He sent Esau a gift of many animals and then spent the night in intense prayer.

When he arrived, "Esau ran to meet him, and embraced him, and fell on his neck, and kissed him: and they wept."

(Genesis 33:4) Esau brought 400 men with him because he was intent on killing Jacob and his family.

But **prayer** saved the day. Their relationship was restored and all ended well. What a beautiful story of God's grace and mercy available to those who pray!!

Once our relationship is restored, one of the most important steps we can take is to make a commitment to each other to nourish and cherish that relationship. Following is a "promise" we can make to each other. I would encourage *spouses* to do this. I still have the copy my wife and I signed in 1997. It is a constant reminder of how precious is that special relationship!!

A RELATIONSHIP PROMISE

Realizing that relationships are more important than kingdoms, I am committed to cherish and nourish ours. I will strive to "esteem you as better than myself." I will seek to understand you by learning your temperament, acknowledging your viewpoint, and meeting your personal needs.

I will accept you unconditionally. I will give you the praise and affirmation you deserve. I will express my appreciation for you often and in many ways.

I will always listen to you and communicate honestly and openly with you. I will encourage and support you in all your dreams and goals.

I will love and trust you. I will live my life *for you*!

Since cooperation is necessary for healthy relationships, I ask you to join me in living this promise together. Will you?

_____   _____
                Signature   Date

CHAPTER 5

RELATIONSHIP SKILLS

Proverbs 18:24 says, "A man that hath friends must shew himself friendly...." So, in order to have great relationships, we need to start with **ourselves**.

There are three major obstacles to developing great relationships: **pride**, **selfishness**, and **low self-esteem**. We need to examine ourselves to make sure that we are free of these.

Proverbs 6 lists seven things God hates with **pride** being the first on the list. James 4:6 declares that, "...God *resisteth* the proud, but giveth grace to the humble." Isaiah 14 tells the story of Lucifer being kicked out of heaven due to his pride. Nobody wants to be around proud people, not even God Himself.

We find this shocking truth in Proverbs 13:10, "*Only* by **pride** cometh *contention*...." Every argument, fight, divorce, church split, and war was and is the result of *pride*!!! No wonder we can't build relationships with pride in our lives!!

If pride is the major source of our relationship problems, then humility offers the key to resolution. The word humility is derived from the Latin word *humus*, which is the organic material in soil that makes it *fertile*. The fruit of the Spirit (godly characteristics) flourishes in the rich soil of humility. Just as salt enhances the flavor of food, humility augments the essence of all virtues.

Thomas Aquinas dubbed *humility*, the "queen of virtues." Consequently, God's Word **commands** us to be "clothed with humility." (First Peter 5:5)

Selfishness is the second obstacle in developing relationships. Selfishness basically says, "I am more important than you!" We would be wise to follow Mary Kay's advice concerning others. She says, "When I meet someone, I try to imagine him wearing an invisible sign that says: **MAKE ME**

FEEL IMPORTANT! I respond to this sign immediately, and it works wonders." (Ash 15)

Low self-esteem is the third obstacle in developing relationships. We must understand that there is a vast difference between low self-esteem and humility. An humble person doesn't think of himself at all, but rather he thinks of others. However, a person with low self-esteem thinks of himself *constantly*, but his thoughts are negative. He sees himself as inferior to others, and often feels inadequate about facing life.

The critical issue concerning relationships is that he tends to view others as he views himself. If he doesn't feel good about himself, neither will he feel good about others. And if he doesn't value himself, he automatically assumes that others won't value him either. It is as if he lives with an aura of negativity that repels others.

As Christians, our value comes from who we are "in Christ." We are not who we once were. The devil wants us to keep looking at what we were without Christ. But look what God says, " ...Be not deceived: neither fornicators, nor idolaters, nor adulterers, nor effeminate, nor abusers of themselves with mankind, nor thieves, nor covetous, nor drunkards, nor revilers, nor extortioners, shall inherit the kingdom of God. And **SUCH WERE SOME OF YOU**: *but* ye are **washed**, *but* ye are **sanctified**, *but* ye are **justified** in the name of the Lord Jesus, and by the Spirit of our God." (First Corinthians 6:9-11)

Once we are humble, generous, and self-assured, we are ready to build healthy relationships. The process is really simple; **just help others feel good about themselves**. Help enhance their self-esteem. Just as low self-esteem is **NOT** *humility*, neither is good self-esteem *pride*!! Self-esteem is simply being confident in who you are as a person.

Since God made us in His *image*, we have **infinite potential**. He looks beyond our seeming deficiencies and failures to see what we can become. Abram was childless but God changed his name to Abraham (*father of a multitude*) and he fathered the nation of Israel.

Building relationships begins with **ACCEPTANCE**! George Washington said, "We must make the best of mankind as they are, since we cannot have them as we wish."

The Bible asks this question, "Can the Ethiopian change his skin, or the leopard his spots...?" (Jeremiah 13:23) Some people don't like the way they are, but find it difficult to change. However, God is able to change people, but until He does, we must *accept* them in their present condition. Listen to God's plea for all to come to Him just as they are, "*Come now...* though your sins be as scarlet, they shall be as white as snow; though they be red like crimson, they shall be as wool." (Isaiah 1:18)

A preacher once asked a young lady if she had peace with God. Her answer was that she wanted to get her life cleaned up first. He responded by saying, "Come just as you are." That day she trusted Christ to save her. Her name was Charlotte Elliott. She subsequently wrote about 150 hymns, with the most famous being **JUST AS I AM**.

Billy Graham used this hymn extensively in his crusades because, according to him, it presented "the strongest Biblical basis for the Call of Christ." Kenneth Osbeck, having written sixteen books related to hymn stories and music ministry is considered an expert on the history of hymnology. He wrote that *JUST AS I AM* has "touched more hearts and influenced more people for Christ than any other song ever written."

Another important relationship builder is **APPROVAL**. Approval goes beyond acceptance. We look for positive *virtues*, *actions*, and *attitudes* in others, and compliment accordingly.

Mark Twain said he could live for three weeks on a compliment. A compliment is basically emotional support. Since we are more *psychological* than *logical*, compliments are good for the soul.

Andrew Carnegie had great insight in dealing with people. He said, "Men are developed the same way gold is mined. When gold is mined, several tons of dirt must be moved to get an ounce of gold, but one doesn't go into the mine looking for dirt - one goes in looking for the gold."

Dirt is *apparent*, but gold isn't. So, if you want to enhance your relationships, become a personality gold digger - looking for the **best** in others!!

In Philippians 4:8, Paul mentions eight positive things we are to think about. We could make a similar list of positive things to look for in others.

William James, the father of American psychology, said, "The deepest principle in human nature is the *craving* to be **APPRECIATED**." He didn't speak, mind you, of the "wish" or the "desire" or the "longing" to be appreciated. He said the "craving" to be appreciated. Dale Carnegie said, "Here is a gnawing and unfaltering human hunger, and the *rare* individual who honestly satisfies this heart hunger will hold people in the palm of his or her hand and "even the undertaker will be sorry when he dies." (McGinnis 99-100)

Expressing **APPRECIATION** is a very powerful people skill, as is obvious from the quotes of William James and Dale Carnegie. However, gratitude must be *cultivated* - it is **NOT** a natural trait of mankind. The following Biblical story proves this point.

Leprosy was a dreadful disease in Biblical times. It was so feared by society that social distancing was mandated. And there was no cure apart from divine healing.

Luke tells the story of ten lepers healed by Jesus. Only one thanked Him for his miraculous healing. "And Jesus answering said, were there not ten cleansed? But where are the nine? There are not found that returned to give glory to God, save this stranger." (Luke 17:17-18)

This is a sad commentary concerning the ungrateful

condition of the human heart. First Thessalonians 5:18 implies that a spirit of gratitude is to be our *lifestyle*. So, we would be wise to continually practice the art of expressing gratitude. It is indispensble in building healthy relationships!!

As a matter of fact, gratitude is such a *bonding* emotion that many scientists have deemed it the psychological "glue" that keeps people *close*! No wonder the devil works overtime to keep us from being grateful.

Practicing **RECOGNITION** is another important element in our relationships. Remember, we are trying to help others feel good about themselves. How people think about themselves is usually a *reflection* of what others think about them.

The desire for *social distinction* is common in man. A.J. Snow says, "Desiring to be well thought of and knowing that everyone we come into contact with cannot possibly be acquainted with us intimately, we learn to rely to a great extent upon *external objects* to testify to our worth."

Football players have stars/stickers on their helmets representing their best plays. Soldiers wear medals indicating their service achievements. Philanthropists have *hospitals* and *libraries* named after them.

Most of us cannot do things at this level, but we can remember birthdays, anniversaries, and other important events with a phone call, card, or text. This means a lot to those you are recognizing.

Remembering names is a crucial element in recognition. All of us enjoy hearing our own name spoken. Henry Ward Beecher said, "A man's name takes hold of a thousand inward chords, and may be so pronounced that almost every nerve and sensibility of his being shall be thrilled by it."

Many years ago I was talking with a lady at church. I don't remember the gist of the conversation, but suddenly she said, "My name is ____." Evidently I was not calling her by name during the conversation. She had low self-esteem and just needed to hear her name. I learned a valuable lesson that day. Now, during conversations, I say the person's name.

The Bible has a lot to say about **ENCOURAGEMENT** because all of us need it. We should memorize and meditate on Isaiah 50:4, "The Lord hath given me the tongue of the learned, that I should know how to speak a *word in season* to him that is *weary*...." God wants us to be encouragers.

Jesus started His earthly ministry as an encourager: "The Spirit of the Lord is upon me, because he hath anointed me to preach the gospel to the *poor*; he hath sent me to heal the *brokenhearted*, to preach deliverance to the *captives*, and recovering of sight to the blind, to set at liberty them that are *bruised*." (Luke 4:18) Listen to His plea to all of us, "Come unto me, all ye that labour and are **heavy laden**, and I will give you rest." (Matthew 11:28)

Observe how He equips us for this ministry. "Blessed be God, even the Father of our Lord Jesus Christ, the Father of mercies, and the **GOD OF ALL COMFORT**; who *comforteth* us in **all** our *tribulation*, **that** we may be able to *comfort* them which are in *trouble*, **by** the *comfort* wherewith we ourselves are *comforted* of God." (Second Corinthians 1:3-4)

The Greek word for comfort means "to call near, especially for help." It is also translated as encouragement and as consolation. So, God calls us near to Him to encourage us, and comfort us when we are experiencing a tough time. Then we will be able to encourage others the same way God encouraged us.

Several years ago, God said to me, "You will reap **IF** you don't faint." At the time, I did not understand what this meant, but for the next two years I went through living hell. Satan assaulted me, my family, and the church I pastored. I was actually living Daniel 7:25 which says that the devil tries to "wear out the saints."

I got to the point where I was physically, emotionally, mentally, and spiritually *exhausted*! Back then, I didn't know anything about taking a sabbatical, but I knew I had to get away for a while. My wife and I drove about 45 miles to DeRidder, Louisiana, to spend the night. But none of the motels had a vacancy. So, we drove another 20 or so miles to Leesville.

I woke up about 4:00 A.M. the next morning and knew immediately that I had an appointment with God. I got dressed and just drove around the countryside near Leesville. I can't explain it, but God refreshed me in those early morning hours. By the time I got back to the motel, my exhaustion was gone, my zeal had returned, and the devil was defeated.

As an evangelist, I meet many pastors all over the United States. I have been able to encourage many with the same encouragement God gave me. It is a rewarding ministry - **ENCOURAGEMENT**! God wants to use you in this capacity too!!

TRANSPARENCY is another crucial aspect of healthy relationships. A close personal relationship requires a great degree of *self-disclosure*. No relationship will ever be deeper than our level of *trust*.

At the heart of self-disclosure is sharing your *thoughts* and *emotions*. However, men are much more reluctant to share their feelings than women. G.K. Chesterton addressed this issue when he said that the meanest fear is the fear of *sentimentality*.

Having a clear understanding of the power of self-disclosure, Mary Ann Evans, writing under the pen name of George Eliot, said, "Oh, the comfort, the inexpressible comfort of feeling safe with a person; having neither to weigh thoughts nor measure words but to pour them all out, just as it is, chaff and grain together, knowing that a faithful friend will take and sift them, keeping what is worth keeping, and then, with the breath of kindness blow the rest away." (McGinnis 36)

In his book, *The Transparent Self*, psychologist Sidney Jourard suggests that the human personality has a natural *desire* for self-disclosure. But when that desire is **NOT** fulfilled, **emotional problems** arise.

Proverbs 28:13 says, "He that *covereth* his sins shall **not** prosper: but whoso *confesseth* and *forsaketh* them shall have mercy." We must be honest with God, for He already knows everything about us.

Once Jesus revealed that He knew her past, the Samaritan woman was joyously set free. She left her waterpot, ran to the city, and told the men, "Come, see a man, which told me **all things** that ever I did: is not this the Christ?" (John 4:29)

Satan's kingdom is one of darkness (Colossians 1:13). And every bit of darkness in your heart is harmful to you - *emotionally* and *physically*. The Biblical *command* is to "**Confess** your *faults* one to another, and pray one for another that ye may be **healed** (*to make whole*)!" (James 5:16) So, self-disclosure is very *therapeutic*!!

Self-disclosure also produces the power of **attraction**. The dynamic involved here is reciprocity, the basic premise of which is: self-disclosure begets self-disclosure. (Greenfield 39)

Transparency fosters friendship. When we remove our masks, others are drawn to us. However, we must use wisdom in this area and leave the results to God. There may be some things in our past that need to remain there, unless God prompts us to share. But overall, transparency is the only path to deeper relationships!! Remember, our relationships remain at the level of our *trust*.

Communication is the life-blood of relationships, but **LISTENING** is the key component. Listening goes far beyond hearing audible sounds. It includes the more intricate psychological process of *interpreting* and *understanding* not only *what* is being said, but also *how* and *why*.

The *what* is difficult enough because people don't always mean exactly what we think they are saying. The *how* comes from their *tone of voice* and their *demeanor* at the moment. To catch these critical nuances, we must be paying close attention to them. We can't just listen with our emotions. We must literally feel their emotional energy in some instances to get a clear understanding of what they are saying.

Many years ago I was granted the privilege of spending a week with a well-known professional Christian counselor. I sat in a corner of his office observing as he counseled with each couple. If I felt that I had a worthy insight that might be helpful, I would share it with him during a break and he would determine if I could share it with the couple.

As I listened attentively and observed carefully while he was dealing with one of the couples, the Lord gave me insight concerning their issues. The wife's mom and dad cared for several foster children while she was growing up. When she got married, she wanted to follow in their footsteps and care for foster children also.

However, the husband was not keen on that idea, but she did it anyway. I don't remember him saying anything at all about it. But it was clear to me from the atmosphere of the meeting that was the major problem in their marriage.

I shared it with the counselor and he agreed with me. I don't remember if they arrived at a resolution. What I do remember is that session involved the most intense listening I have ever done.

Listening is the most effective single technique for helping troubled people. And if it helps them, how much more will it help all of our relationships.

Love is at the heart of all relationships, and *true love* listens! Listening is one of the *highest compliments* we can pay someone. Oliver Wendell Holmes said, "To be able to listen to others in a sympathetic and understanding manner is perhaps the most *effective mechanism* in the world for getting along with people and tying up their friendship for good." (Giblin 94)

Learn as much as you can about the art of listening. Then apply this art abundantly. You will be pleasantly surprised as the quality of your relationships begin to soar!!

TOUCH is a *universal* language. It performs a level of caring beyond all other forms of communication.

It communicates *warmth* and *affirmation*. "Then there were brought unto him little children, that he should put his hands on them, and pray... And he laid his hands on them." (Matthew 19:13-15) The disciples rebuked the parents for doing this, but Jesus said, "Suffer little children, and forbid them not, to come unto me...." Little children **need** the caring, loving touch of those who love them.

Touching also symbolizes *acceptance*. In Matthew 8:3, Jesus touched a leper which was unheard of in those days. And with that touch, the leper was healed. In Matthew 8:15, Jesus touched the hand of Peter's sick mother-in-law and she was instantly healed. We see this healing touch repeatedly in the New Testament.

In Mark 5, a woman touched the hem of Jesus' garment and was immediatley healed. Then Jesus asked who touched Him because He felt *virtue* go out of Him. The Greek word for virtue is *dynamis* which means strength, ability, and miraculous power. Miraculous power can come from a simple touch. So, touch also represents *transference* of power.

Several years ago I was in Texas teaching a seminar on *Praying for the Lost*. After the morning session, I ate lunch with a couple from the church and spent time with them until the afternoon session.

The lady told me about an Assembly of God church a few miles away that was experiencing a healing revival. As the evangelist walked through the congregation, God would reveal individual issues among the people. He would pray for them and they would be healed. There were many documented healings, confirmed by doctors.

My meeting was at 4:00 P.M., so I had time to teach my seminar and then drive to that church for the evening service. I prayed for God to give the evangelist a "word" for me. I had been having severe back pain for quite some time and driving all over the country preaching really aggravated the problem.

I drove to the church and sat on the front row. After the worship time, the evangelist said, "We are going to do things differently tonight. We have never done it this way before." Then he said, "Everyone with back trouble, please stand up." At that moment I knew God was going to heal me that night.

There were about a dozen of us that stood up. When he laid his hands on me, and prayed, God healed me instantly. After he dealt with all of us, he retired to the pastor's study to rest. Much power had gone out of him!!

I also had sleep apnea. So, I told his wife that I needed him to pray for me again. After a while when he got his energy back, he laid hands on me and prayed again. God healed me of sleep apnea, and I have never used a breathing machine again.

When he laid his hands on me, virtue or power was *transferred* from his hands to my body. There is a real transference of power through touch. Even if it is not the healing power of God coming through, a loving touch still conveys power.

Touching increases your level of dopamine and seratonin, two neurotransmitters that help regulate your mood by reducing stress and anxiety. Touching also helps regulate sleep and digestion, build your immune system, and fight infection. Research has shown that it takes 8-10 meaningful touches a day to maintain physical and emotional health.

Spokesmen for medical science now say that hugging is a miracle medicine capable of relieving many physical and emotional problems. Dr. David Bresler says, "To be **held** is *enormously therapeutic*." Someone said that a hug joins the *physical* and *emotional* so tightly together that they are indistinguishable from each other.

The brain responds to a hug by releasing a hormone called oxytocin. Oxytocin makes us more successful at *forming* and *maintaining* relationships. It is known as the "bonding hormone."

When my wife is not feeling well she comes to me for a hug. There are many people in our sphere of influence that could use a hug from someone who cares. Can you spare a few?

Touching is a powerful way to build healthy relationships. Use it wisely!!

COURTESY is simply courtlike manners; acting with dignity and decorum in the presence of *royalty*. Matthew 25:31-46 is a divine revelation of **HOW** we should treat others. With His skill of simplifying difficult problems, Jesus distills the art of relationships into one sentence. "And the **King** shall answer and say unto them, Verily I say unto you, In as much as ye have done it unto one of the **least** of these my brethren, ye have done it unto me." (Matthew 25:40)

The Greek word for **least** means the smallest in *importance*, in *authority*, in *rank*, in *dignity*, and in the *estimation* of men. So, Jesus **expects** us to treat others as we should treat Him, the Lord of Lords and King of Kings, with dignity and decorum in the presence of **ROYALTY**!!

Ted Engstrom humorously captures the essence of the transforming power of courtlike manners in his story of Joe:

> It seemed that Joe had just about had it with his wife of three years. He no longer thought of her as attractive or interesting; he considered her to be a poor housekeeper who was overweight, someone he no longer wanted to live with. Joe was so upset that he finally decided on divorce. But before he served her the papers, he made an appointment with a psy-

chologist with the specific purpose of finding out how to make life as difficult as possible for his wife.

The psychologist listened to Joe's story and then gave this advice, "Well, Joe, I think I've got the perfect solution for you. Starting tonight when you get home, I want you to start treating your wife as if she were a goddess. That's right, a goddess. I want you to change your attitude toward her 180 degrees. Start doing everything in your power to please her. Listen intently to her when she talks about her problems, help around the house, take her out to dinner on weekends. I want you to literally pretend that she's a goddess. Then, after two months of this wonderful behavior, just pack your bags and leave her. That should get to her!"

Joe thought it was a tremendous idea. That night he started treating his wife as if she were a goddess. He couldn't wait to do things for her. He brought her breakfast in bed and had flowers delivered to her for no apparent reason. Within three weeks the two of them had gone on two romantic weekend vacations. They read books to each other at night, and Joe listened to her as never before. It was incredible what Joe was doing for his wife. He kept it up for the full two months. After the allotted time, the psychologist gave Joe a call at work.

"Joe," he asked, "how's it going? Did you file for divorce? Are you a happy bachelor once again?"

"Divorce?" asked Joe in dismay. "Are

you kidding? I'm married to a goddess. I've never been happier in my life. I'd never leave my wife in a million years. In fact, I'm discovering new, wonderful things about her every single day. Divorce? Not on your life."

Proverbs 17:22 says, "A merry heart doeth good like a medicine...." The outward evidence of a merry heart is a **SMILE**. Your smile may be the medicine someone needs; so, be generous with yours.

A smile is an instant *invitation* to a relationship. Les Giblin said, "A real, sincere smile works almost like a *magic switch* that turns on a friendly feeling in the other fellow *instantly*." Dorothy Dix declared that, "There is no other weapon in the whole feminine armory to which men are so vulnerable as they are to a smile."

Harvey Ball first drew the "smiley face" in 1963. But Franklin Loufrani registered the symbol in 1971 and holds the trademark in much of the world. The Smiley Company's annual revenue is about $500 million.

Ball never sought a trademark or copyright; he just wants recognition as smiley's creator. He said, "Never in the history of mankind or art has any single piece of art gotten such widespread *favor*, *pleasure*, or *enjoyment*. And nothing has ever been so **simply done** and so **easily understood** in art." What a testimony to a simple smile!!

Through the Smiley Company, we have seen the value of a smile. But the financial aspect is limited to just a few. However, the real value of a smile is *limitless* for **ALL**!!

The Value of a Smile

- It cost nothing, but creates much.
- It enriches those who receive, without impoverishing those who give.
- It happens in a flash, and the memory of it some times lasts forever.
- None are so rich they can get along without it, and none so poor but are richer for its benefits.
- It creates happiness in the home, fosters good will in business, and is the countersign of friends.
- It is rest to the weary, cheer to the discouraged, sunshine to the sad, and nature's best antidote for trouble.
- Yet it cannot be bought, begged, borrowed, or stolen, for it is something that is no earthly good to anybody `til it is given away!
- Nobody needs a smile so much as those who have none left to give!

Author Unknown

Smiles are priceless!! So, be generous with yours. Make this a part of your relationship skill set.

> "It was only a sunny smile,
> and little it cost in giving,
> but like the morning light
> it scattered the night and
> made the day worth living."

F. Scott Fitzgerald

We should always be **GENTLE** with others. We are to "Speak evil of no man...but *gentle*, shewing all *meekness* unto **all men**." (Titus 3:2) Paul doubles up on gentleness in this verse because meekness is a special kind of gentleness.

A meek person is one with great inner strength, but because of his submission to God, is outwardly calm and gentle. This is especially true when dealing with difficult people or situations. The most frequent Biblical context concerning the meek refers to their reward for patient endurance.

When this same Greek verb for meek refers to animals, it is translated as "tame." A tame horse is submissive to its master, but still retains its strength.

In the mid-17th century, James Watt experimented with horses hauling coal out of coal mines. He concluded that a horse can do 33,000 foot-pounds of work per minute, which equates to one horsepower. How much horsepower does your car have?

Being gentle with people could change their lives. In Second Samuel 22:36, David said, "Thy **gentleness** hath made me *great*." In his transformation from a shepherd to Israel's most beloved king, David cites God's **gentleness** with him as the major factor.

Paul Daily founded "Wild Horse Ministries" in 1997, near Jena, Louisiana. In taming a wild horse, he demonstrates how God deals with us in drawing us to salvation.

His website states, "Paul does not 'break horses,' he **'gentles'** them, with words and pats, until they let him bridle, saddle, and ride them - all within two hours. Occasionally, Paul can get the horses to totally submit by lying down."

Just think, if Paul Daily can totally tame a wild horse in two hours, through **GENTLENESS** alone, how much more could we do for people by being gentle with them. In employing every *people skill* we can, let's place *gentleness* near the top!!

We must never forget that first and foremost, we are *spiritual beings*. Therefore, **PRAYING** for each other is one of the most important things we can do. S.D. Gordon said, "The *greatest* thing anyone can do for God and for man is to pray. It is not the only thing. But it is the *chief* thing...You can do more than pray, **after** you have prayed. But you can not do more than pray until you have prayed." (Gordon 12-16)

Nick Saban is undoubtedly the GOAT of college football coaches, having won seven national championships. He stressed *discipline* and *excellence.*

Excellence is the fruit of discipline. First Corinthians 9:23 says, "And every man that striveth for the mastery is *temperate* in **ALL** things. Now they do it to obtain a corruptible crown; but we an incorruptible." Temperate means to be disciplined.

If we are to build great relationships, we need to *practice* relationship skills. I recommend making a list of these skills, and practice, practice, practice until they become second nature to you.

CHAPTER 6

VALUING RELATIONSHIPS

Billy Graham was perhaps God's greatest statesman of modern history. The breadth and depth of his influence was apparent by his lying in state in the United States Capital rotunda. At the time, he was one of only thirty people to have had this honor bestowed upon them.

At his funeral, many moving accolades were expressed. However, for me, the greatest and the most revealing tribute came from his daughter, Ruth. She told how she had gone through a heart-rending relationship failure.

Broken, she headed to her parent's home, unsure about their reception. She said, "As I rounded the last bend in my father's driveway, Daddy was waiting for me. He wrapped his arms around me and said, "Welcome home." For Ruth, this simple loving reception by her earthly father made him more like our Heavenly Father than any other thing in his life.

God is love (First John 4:8), and as human beings made in God's image, we have a deep desire to be loved. And, as Ruth discovered, to be loved *unconditionally* is immensely therapeutic. Since love "covereth **all** sins" (Proverbs 10:12), it also has the power to relieve us of the *shame*, the *guilt*, and the *degradation* we experience when we sin or feel like failures.

Since love is primarily expressed through **relationships**, it behooves us to hold them in high esteem. Viewing relationships from a biblical perspective quickly reveals their true value.

Above all, God made us in His image in order to have a relationship with us. Then, He sent Christ to die for us, making possible an *intimate* relationship as His children. Although a relationship with God is the most important relationship we can have, the scope of this book deals primarily with our relationships with each other.

God created the earth and all that pertains to it to provide a wonderful living environment for Adam. But, there was one very serious missing link. God said it like this, "It is not good that the man should be **alone**; I will make an *helpmeet* (to aid, to succour, to assist) for him." (Genesis 2:18)

All relationships revolve around needs being met. That is why God said that is was not good for the man to be alone. All of us have needs requiring others to be involved in our lives. The wise man expressed it thusly, "Two are better than one; because they have a good reward for their labour. For if they fall, the one will lift up his fellow; but woe to him that is alone when he falleth; for he hath not another to help him up. Again, if two lie together, then they have heat: but how can one be warm alone? And if one prevail against him, two shall withstand him; and a threefold cord is not quickly broken." (Ecclesiastes 4:9-12)

Although all of us have many *physical* and *psychological* needs, the need to love and to be loved surpasses them all. Love not only covers a *multitude* of **sins** (First Peter 4:8), it also meets a *multitude* of **needs**.

Unexpressed love results in loneliness, which, in turn, produces myriads of problems. Several studies show that continual loneliness causes accelerated aging with multiple health issues that could lead to death.

In his sermon on *Loneliness*, Billy Graham said, "Loneliness is one of the greatest problems people face today. It is a leading cause of suicide - that is now the third greatest killer of students in the United States."

In expressing the supreme value of relationships, Jesus reveals that **ONLY** *God* and *people* are important. He basically summed up the entire Bible by saying, "Thou shalt love the Lord thy God with all thy heart, and with all thy soul, and with all thy mind. This is the first and great commandment. And the second is like unto it, Thou shalt love thy neighbour as thyself. On these two commandments hang all the law and the prophets." (Matthew 22:37-40) Although we tend to pursue **FUN**, **FORTUNE**, and **FAME**, with all of their trappings, **RELATIONSHIPS** should be our top *priority*.

RELATIONSHIP RULES

In the Old Tetstament, God gave us the **TEN COMMANDMENTS** which are basically relationship rules. The first four deal with our relationship with God, while the other six deal with our relationship with people. In the New Testament, He gives some more rules to help us *enhance* our people skills.

The first rule, found in Matthew 25, promises us eternal blessings and is so simple it defies all argument. Therefore, I call this the **PREEMINENT** rule of relationships. In this passage Jesus says, "For **I** was an hungred, and ye gave **me** meat: **I** was thirsty, and ye gave **me** drink: **I** was a stranger, and ye took **me** in...." Eleven times Jesus uses the personal pronouns I and me.

Then the righteous respond with, "Lord, when saw we thee an hungred, and fed thee? or thirsty, and gave thee drink?..." The amazing answer was, "Inasmuch as ye have done it unto one of the least of these my brethren, ye have done it unto **me**." Treating **EVERY** person we meet as if that person is Jesus would change our lives and their lives, and the Lord would be well-pleased!!

Another crucial relationship rule is the **GOLDEN** rule! Matthew 7:12 says, "Therefore all things whatsoever ye would that men should do to you, do ye even so to them: for this is the law and the prophets." We are to treat others in every way, and at all times just like we want to be treated.

Notice the proactive status: we are to do it *first*. For example, husbands, if you want your wife to treat you like a king, start treating her like a queen. If we take the initiative to treat all of our relationships in positive ways, they will become much richer and more rewarding.

Philippians 2:3-4 gives us what I like to call the **PLAT-INUM** rule: "Let nothing be done through strife or vainglory; but in lowliness of mind let each esteem other better than themselves. Look not every man on his own things, but every man also on the things of others."

I want to point out three important truths in these verses. First of all, not a single one of us should do anything whatsoever through strife (self-seeking) or vainglory (empty pride) because **ALL** relationship problems are birthed in **PRIDE**. Proverbs 13:10 says, "**ONLY** by *pride* cometh *contention....*" Secondly, each of us is to *esteem* (consider, deem) each other *better* (to be superior in rank, authority, power) than ourselves. Thirdly, we are to be more concerned with the needs of others than we are with our own.

Another relationship rule is the **ROYAL** law found in James 2:8-9, "If ye fulfill the royal law according to the scripture, Thou shalt love thy neighbour as thyself, ye do well: But if ye have respect to persons, ye commit sin...."

According to Jesus, *neighbour* includes everyone we know or happen to meet regardless of nationality or religion. He didn't just say, "Accept them," which is hard enough, but He said, "Love them as you love yourself."

If this wasn't difficult enough, He really takes us beyond our comfort zone by saying, "Love your *enemies*, bless them that curse you, do good to them that hate you, and pray for them which despitefully use you; **THAT** ye may be the children of your Father which is in heaven: for he maketh **HIS** sun to rise on the evil and on the good, and sendeth rain on the just and on the unjust." (Matthew 5:44-45)

I am sure this is called the **ROYAL** law because God Himself lives by it. Therefore, He expects us to live by it because the salvation of souls is vastly more important than any offense we may face!!

Obeying the royal law includes being *impartial*!! Acts 10:34 tells us that "God is no respecter of persons." He loves the whole world and wants to redeem every single person. Since we are His *children* and His *ambassadors* representing Him on earth, He wants us to do the same.

Proverbs 18:19 says, "A brother offended is harder to be won than a strong city: and their contentions are like the bars of a castle." Many times our actions and attitudes toward others turn them off to the Gospel, which is an eternal tragedy.

ONE ANOTHER COMMANDS

Things we value are usually treated accordingly. For example, a new vehicle owner may use two parking spaces to keep someone from dinging the doors. God has made it perfectly clear in the Bible that we are to value our relationships.

Consequently, the New Testament is full of "one another" passages revealing *how* we are to treat others, especially brothers and sisters in Christ. These should encourage us to be continually sensitive concerning our relationships. The following "one another" passages are actually written as **commands** to be obeyed.

- (First Peter 1:22) "*Love* one another with a pure heart fervently." Loving one another is so important, it is repeated at least a dozen times.

- (James 5:16) "*Pray* for one another, that ye may be healed." Praying for each other is one of the most powerful and effective things we can do.

- (First Thessalonians 5:11) "*Edify* one another." Here, the Lord commands us to build each other up, promoting spiritual growth and well-being.

- (Galatians 5:13) "*Serve* one another." The Greek word for serve is *doulos*, which means a slave. So, we are to serve others while disregarding our own interests. In other words, we are to put others first.

- (James 5:16) "*Confess* your faults one to another." Confess means to acknowledge openly and joyfully. Transparency is good for the soul, for if we cover our sins, we shall not prosper. (Proverbs 28:13)

- (Ephesians 4:32) "Be ye *kind* one to another." The idea here is to be kind and gracious as opposed to being harsh and bitter.

- (Hebrews 3:13) "*Exhort* one another daily." The Greek word is *parakaleo* which means to "call to one's side." The purpose is to encourage, to strengthen, to comfort, and to pray. Perhaps, there is nothing quite so comforting as having friends or loved ones put their arms around us to pray for us and to encourage us during difficult times.

- (Romans 15:7) "*Receive* ye one another as Christ also received us." Just as Christ took us to Himself, so are we to do likewise with others. This carries the idea of granting one access to your heart.

- (Second Corinthians 13:12) "*Greet* one another with an holy kiss." In this context, greet means to enfold in the arms or to embrace. Here in the South, we would say "hug" one another.

ONE ANOTHER PASSAGES

There are many other "one another" passages that are not written as *commands*, but since they are part of the Word of God, we should always obey them.

- (Ephesians 4:2) "*Forbearing* one another in love."All of us have times when things aren't going well, which tend to make us difficult to be around. Hence, we need others to be patient with us, to bear with us, just to put up with us for a while.

- (Ephesians 4:32) "*Forgiving* one another." The root word of forgive is *charis* (grace). To forgive is to show one grace, kindness, favour, and mercy.

- (Ephesians 5:21) "*Submitting* yourselves one to another." This was a military term for arranging troops under the command of a leader. Our attitude should be one of voluntarily submitting to and cooperating with each other.

- (Hebrews 10:24) "*Consider* one another." This means "to observe fully." We are to seek to *understand* others. Many of our relationship problems arise from simple misunderstandings which could have been prevented had we made the effort to see their point of view.

- (Romans 15:14) "*Admonish* one another." The word literally means "to put in mind," or "to call attention to." This could include a warning about something or counseling someone concerning a particular situation.

- (Hebrews 10:24) "Consider one another to *provoke* unto love and to good works." We are to stir up or inspire others until their zeal burns fervently for the things of God.

- (First Peter 4:9) "Use *hospitality* one to another." We are to express warmth, kindness, and generosity to others. This is also one of the qualifications for a bishop (Titus 1:7-8).

- (First Peter 4:10) "As every man hath received the gift even so *minister* the same one to another." We are to use our spiritual gifts to minister to or to serve each other.

- (First John 1:7) "Have *fellowship* one with another." As Christians we are to have continual participation and social interaction with each other. We cannot live in a social vacuum.

SPOUSAL COMMANDS

Since our greatest need is **LOVE** (to love and to be loved), our most significant relationship is with our spouse. God formed all the beasts and birds out of the ground, but He made Eve out of Adam's rib. Adam's response was, "This is now bone of my bones, and flesh of my flesh: she shall be called Woman, because she was taken out of man. Therefore shall a man leave his father and his mother, and shall cleave unto his wife: and they shall be **one flesh**." (Genesis 2:23-24)

Ephesians 5:22-33 likens the husband/wife relationship to that of the Christ/Church relationship. In this passage husbands are *commanded* to **love** their wives as "Christ also loved the church, and gave himself for it."

In this same passage wives are *commanded* to **submit**

themselves to their own husbands. **Submit** is a military term referring to troops under the command of a leader. God gives His chain of command in First Corinthians 11:3, "The head of every *man* is **Christ**; and the head of the *woman* is the **man**; and the head of *Christ* is **God**!"

When this chain of command is broken, *anarchy* reigns. Anarchy comes from the Greek prefix "an" (*without*) and the Greek noun "archou" (*ruler*). It literally means "without a ruler."

There are two compelling reasons why God commands wives to be subject to their own husbands. First, disobedience constitutes rebellion, and "Rebellion is as the sin of *witchcraft*, and stubborness is iniquity and *idolatry*." (First Samuel 15:23) Thus, rebellion in the home opens the door to demonic activity. I believe this is one of the primary reasons for so many broken homes and for the destruction of so many young people in our society today.

The other reason why wives are to be subject to their husbands is because this is a crucial element in the conversion of lost husbands (First Peter 3:1-6). Wives must trust God to save their husbands which will not work if they are in a state of rebellion. God encourages wives to follow the pattern set by holy women of old. They were in subjection to their husbands *because* they "trusted in God" (First Peter 3:5-6).

He then gives the intriguing example of Sara; "Even as Sara obeyed Abraham, calling him Lord." Twice, not once, but twice Abraham gave Sara over to wicked kings for their sexual pleasure. And Sara still called him "lord." How could she do this? Because she "trusted in God" and each time God rebuked the kings with severe warnings if they even touched her.

Sara's faith was **NOT** in her husband, rather her faith was in God. This is also how God intends for us to operate in our spousal relationships. He can handle situations that seem totally hopeless to us if we will let Him.

Another valuable truth about spousal relationships is that they are so important to God that He makes them a *condition* of **answered prayer** (First Peter 3:7). If the husband/wife relationship is that important to God, surely it should be important to us also.

POWER OF LOVE

If we live the truths of First Corinthians 13, we will not have relationship problems. The first eight verses basically summarizes the power of love.

Paul personalizes the first three verses by using the personal pronouns I, me, and my eleven times. He also lists seven very powerful aspects of the Christian life: tongues of men and angels, prophecy, understanding mysteries, knowledge, faith, generosity, and sacrifice. Then he takes five of these to the *nth* degree: understanding **ALL** mysteries, having **ALL** knowledge, **ALL** faith, giving away **ALL** my goods, and giving **MY** body to be burned.

Can you even imagine what it would be like to personally know someone who understands **ALL** mysteries? He/she could answer any question and help you understand *why* concerning any issue. What about someone with **ALL** faith who could move *every* mountain, and heal *every* person of any disease?

And now imagine how wonderful it would be to know someone who had **ALL** of these godly powers and characteristics. Paul concludes by admitting that even if *he* had all these graces to the *nth* degree, but did not have love, he would be nothing. The bottom line is, *without* **LOVE**, *none of these things matter*. The lack of love renders all of these powerful spiritual features completely worthless.

And now, read for yourself the marvelous qualities of love found in verses 4-8, but concentrate for a while on these,

"*Beareth* **ALL** things, *believeth* **ALL** things, *hopeth* **ALL** things, *endureth* **ALL** things. Charity (love) **NEVER** *faileth*!" Allow these five unsurpassing aspects of love to sink into your heart and you will discover this wonderful truth: *with* **LOVE**, *nothing else matters*. Regardless of how difficult your life and your relationships may become, **LOVE** always *overcomes*!!

Notice one other truth concerning the power of love. The Lord lists *faith*, *hope*, and *love* as the three enduring spiritual aspects of life. Both faith and hope are essential for our own physical and spiritual well-being. Faith is so important that it is a requirement for getting things from God (Matthew 9:29); nor can we please Him without it (Hebrews 11:6). Furthermore, God wants us to *abound* in hope (Romans 15:13).

What then, makes love so much greater than faith and hope? Because faith and hope are for *ourselves*, but love is for *others*. Love is the **ESSENCE** of relationships, making it far superior to both faith and hope.

We have been discussing the value and the importance of our relationships. However, all of us would agree that some of our relationships are more important than others. Perhaps none of us *express* love as often as we should or to as many as we should, making it impossible to discern the depth of some relationships. With this in mind, consider this quote from G.K. Chesterton, "To the world, you may be just *one person*, but to one person, you may be *the world*."

CHAPTER 7

THE ULTIMATE RELATIONSHIP

The ultimate relationship concerns **eternity**!! There are two **MASSIVE** eternal issues about which we must be aware - *where* and *how*.

Where will you spend eternity? This is the most important question you will ever face. There are only two options - **HEAVEN** or **HELL**!!!

If you have a relationship with the Lord Jesus Christ, heaven will be your eternal home. However, if you do not have a relationship with Christ, hell will be your eternal abode.

You can establish a relationship with Christ in **three** easy steps.

1. **Realize** that you are a sinner sentenced to eternal death. Romans 5:12 says, "Wherefore, as by one man sin entered into the world, and *death* by sin; and so *death* passed upon *all* men, for that *all* have sinned."

2. **Accept** by faith God's *gift* of eternal life provided by Christ through His death on the cross. Romans 6:23 says, "For the wages of sin is death; but the *gift* of God is **eternal life** *through* Jesus Christ our Lord."

3. **Pray** a simple prayer *confessing* Christ as your Lord and Saviour while *believing* in your heart that He died for you and that God raised Him from the dead. Romans 10:9-10 says, "That if thou shalt *confess* with thy mouth the Lord Jesus, and shalt *believe* in thine heart that God hath raised him from the dead, thou shalt be saved. For with the *heart man believeth* unto righteousness; and with the mouth confession is made unto salvation."

There are many religions in the world, but religion can't save you. Religion is man looking for God, but Christianity is God looking for man. Luke 19:10 declares that, "The *Son of man* is come to *seek* and to *save* that which was lost."

Religionists are seeking an *amoral* god, that's why they can't find **THE GOD**!! In John 3:19, Jesus said, "And this is the condemnation, that light is come into the world, and men *loved darkness* rather than light, **BECAUSE** their *deeds were evil*."

Even in the end times God's Word tells of men who "repented not of the works of their hands, that they should not worship devils, and idols of gold, and silver, and brass, and stone, and of wood: which neither can see, nor hear, nor walk." (Revelation 9:20) Mankind wants a god, but **NOT** one that will convict them of their sins. And they find that in **RELIGION**!!!

Here is a small sampling of Scriptures proclaiming that a relationship with Christ is the **ONLY** way to have eternal life.

- (Acts 4:12) "Neither is there salvation in any other: for there is none other name under heaven given among men, **whereby we must be saved**."

- (John 1:12) "But as many as received him, to them gave he **power to become the sons of God**, even to them that believe on his name."

- (First John 5:11-12) "And this is the record, that God hath given to us *eternal life*, and *this life is in his Son*. **He that hath the Son**, *hath life*; and he that hath **NOT** the Son of God hath not life."

- (John 3:36) "**He that believeth on the Son hath everlasting life**; and he that believeth **NOT** the Son shall not see life; but the wrath of God abideth on him."

The next issue is *how* will we spend eternity. If you refuse a relationship with Christ, then your *how* will be continual torment in a lake of fire and brimstone. That is a terrible way to spend eternity!

But if you are a Christian, your *how* will be determined by your **service** to the Lord Jesus Christ. Obviously, God blesses His people here on earth as we serve Him, but I am talking about *eternal* blessings.

The greatest of all blessings is being able to spend eternity in *heaven* with the Lord Jesus. Read Revelation 21 for a glimpse of heaven and its glory.

The second blessing will be *rewards*. Several Scriptures speak of our eternal rewards (Luke 6:23), (First Corinthians 3:8), (Revelation 22:12). They have to do with our service to Him. Matthew 16:27 sums it up, "For the Son of man shall come in the glory of his Father with his angels; and then he shall **reward** every man *according to his works*."

The third blessing will be *crowns*. Second Timothy 4:8 mentions a "crown of righteousness," James 1:12 mentions a "crown of life," and First Peter 5:4 mentions a "crown of glory."

The Olympic Games began in the 7th Century BC, in Olympia, Greece. Several times Paul made reference to these games in the New Testament. In First Corinthians 9:25, he describes the disciplined and strenuous training needed to win the crown. "And every man that striveth for the mastery is temperate in all things. Now they do it to obtain a corruptible **crown**; but we an *incorruptible*."

The entire passage of First Corinthians 9:24-27 refers to

the Olympic Games. Their training was primarily physical and mental. But our training for God's work is spiritual. It is a battle between the *spirit* and the *flesh*. Paul said, "But I keep under my body, and bring it into subjection: lest that by any means, when I have preached to others, I myself should be a castaway." Castaway means unfit or unworthy of the prize.

The fourth blessing is the most glorious of all. I call it our eternal, spiritual **LEGACY**. It is based on soul-winning.

Proverbs 11:30 tells us that, "The *fruit* of the righteous is a tree of life; and he that *winneth souls is wise*." Couple this with Daniel 12:3, "And they that be *wise* shall shine as the brightness of the firmament; and they that **turn many to righteousness as the stars for ever and ever**."

God created mankind in order to have a relationship with us throughout eternity. Christ died on the cross to secure that relationship. So, there is no wonder that our eternal legacy as Christians will be based on the winning of souls.

In 2022, over 67 million people died. That is over 183,000 daily. It is estimated that less than 12 percent of the world's poplulation have a personal relationship with Christ. That means approximately 160,000 people went to hell **EVERY SINGLE DAY** last year. So, as God's people, we aren't doing a very good job of winning souls.

I want to suggest four fundamental things that we can do that will be productive in the winning of souls, thus ensuring our eternal legacy. First and foremost we should follow the last instruction of Jesus to his disciples concerning **being filled with the Holy Spirit** (Acts 1:4-8). When we are filled with the Spirit, we "*shall be witnesses*" unto Him (Acts 1:8).

Only the Holy Spirit can give us the *power* and *boldness* we need to be soul-winners. I can't even imagine anyone being as bashful and shy as me. Yet, when God filled me with His Spirit in Key West, Florida, in 1969, I was bold enough to stop strangers on Duval Street and tell them about Jesus.

One night I stopped a young man, probably in his early 20's (I was 20 at the time) and started witnessing to him. I guess he came under conviction. Suddenly he turned and started running away. I took off after him and caught him. I continued to tell him about Jesus and he asked the Lord to save him. He went to church with me that Sunday and got baptized. God changed his life! No one who knew me would ever have thought I would have been so bold as to chase a man down to witness to him.

The primary **key** to being a soul-winner is the fulness of the Holy Spirit. Ask the Lord to fill you with His Spirit and **He will**!!

Prayer is also a major key to winning souls. I wrote a book entitled *Praying Effectively for the Lost*. We have over one million copies printed in 36 languages. God has used the book all over the world to help His people win souls. Please contact us for a copy.

Giving financially to soul-winning ministries is another effective way to see souls saved. God raises up *harvesting* ministries, and your financial support helps them bring in the harvest.

Paul wrote to the Philippian Church concerning their financial support to him. He said, "...ye sent once and again unto my necessity. Not because I desire a gift: but I desire *fruit* that may **abound to your account**." (Philippians 4:16-17) They invested in Paul's ministry therefore they shared in his soul-winning *rewards*, and **legacy**.

God blesses some people financially so they can support those He has raised up to bring in the harvest. Luke 8:1-3, tells of several women who "*ministered* unto Jesus of their *substance*." Jesus was responsible for the twelve men who left all to follow Him. He could have turned the sand on the seashore into gold, but He did not. He depended on God's people to help Him do His work. He still does today.

A **godly example** is another way to be effective in winning souls. In his book *Quiet Talks on Prayer*, S.D. Gordon lists five outlets through which the Holy Spirit reveals His power. "First: through the life, **what we are**. Just simply what we are. If we be right the power of God will be constantly flowing out, though we be not conscious of it. It throws the keenest kind of emphasis on a man being right in his life. There will be an eager desire to serve. Yet we may constantly *do more* in **what we are** than in **what we do**. We may serve better in the lives we live than in the best service we ever give." (Gordon 10)

This is exactly what Jesus means in Matthew 5:13-16. He says that we, His people, are the *salt* of the earth and the *light* of the world.

Salt serves as a flavor enhancer for our food, and also as a preservative. Salt is also necessary for maintaining life. Human beings cannot even live without a certain amount of salt. Therefore, some experts believe that our brains tend to crave salt as a life-preserving stimulus.

By declaring that we **are** "the salt of the earth," Jesus intends for us to have a similar affect on the people of the world. He "went about *doing good*, and *healing* all that were oppressed of the devil" (Acts 10:38), in other words, **being salt**!! He wants us to do the same.

We are not just a light in the world, rather we are **the** "light of the world." The purpose is for our Lord to shine so brightly in us and through us that the people of the world will glorify the Father.

A personal relationship with Jesus Christ is the most important relationship we can have. If you do not know Christ as your Saviour, I beg you to take care of that immediately. It is the **ULTIMATE** relationship.

Works Cited

Ash, Mary Kay   *Mary Kay on People Management*, Warner Books, Inc, New York 1984

Giblin, Les   *How to Have Confidence and Power in Dealing with People*, Prentice-Hall, Englewood Cliffs, NJ

Gordon, S. D.   *Quiet Talks on Prayer*, Fleming H. Revell, New York, NY 1904

Greenfield, Guy   *We Need Each Other*, Baker Book House, Grand Rapids, MI 1984

Hallesby, Ole   *Temperament And The Christian Faith*, Augsburg Publishing House, Minneapolis, MN 1962

Heatherly, Joyce   *Balcony People*, Balcony Publishing, Austin, TX 1984

LaHaye, Tim   *Why You Act The Way You Do*, Tyndale, Wheaton, IL 1984

McGinnis, Alan   *The Friendship Factor*, Augsburg Publishing House, Minneapolis, MN